How to S[illegible]tle Company

Operate and Gain Success on Your Own Terms

Author: Maverick Burton

By reading this document, the reader agrees that under no circumstances is the author responsible for any losses, direct or indirect, that are incurred as a result of the use of information contained within this document, including, but not limited to, errors, omissions, or inaccuracies.

Table of Contents

Introduction

Do you want to start your own title company? Is it your ultimate goal to help anyone who intends to buy a property, like a home, and make the entire process easier for them? Do you want to earn a profit while offering such services? Then use this book as a powerful and extensive guide on how to make that happen.

This book aims to inform anyone who wants to start their own title company about the ins and outs of establishing and launching this type of business. You will get to know what you need from the start of the process up until the time when it is already launched and you are already ready to market and expose your business to a lot of people.

It covers even the most effective techniques in marketing and promoting your business to people who can help it grow, like real estate professionals and lenders. Moreover, you will be able to learn about how you can expand your network and your entire business.

Basically, most of the things you intend to know about creating your own title company, making it prosper, and introducing it to your target audience are included here. You will also know how to win and attract potential clients and retain them.

With the aid of this book, you will be guided all throughout the process of starting your own business. It would be like a powerful weapon you could use to get closer to the success you desire in this industry.

Let's start!

Chapter 1 – What Do You Need to Do to Get Started?

Are you thinking of building your own title company and making it stay afloat despite the fierce competition in this industry? Then you have to jumpstart this business endeavor by keeping yourself as well-informed about it as possible. Note that you will not be able to start your title company if you don't have a clear idea of what to do.

In the first chapter of this book, you will get introduced to what a title company is and what it does specifically. By learning about that, you will know exactly how to begin and make your business grow and flourish. You will also be enlightened about the first few but the most important things you need to get started.

What Exactly is a Title Company?

Basically, a title company refers to a third-party company, which you can expect to operate on behalf of the buyer and lender. It is advisable to hire this company if you want professionals to research the title of the property that you intend to buy and insure it.

With the aid of a title company, you have an assurance that you receive a legitimate title to the piece of property or real estate you are buying. It is also responsible for issuing title insurance for such property, which offers protection to the owner and the lender from possible claims or lawsuits against the property caused by title disputes.

You will also find title companies useful in maintaining escrow accounts, the ones containing the funds necessary in closing the home. With the help of these accounts, you have a hundred percent guarantee that the funds or money will be used specifically for closing and settlement costs. It is also the title company that's responsible for conducting a home's formal closing.

During the closing, the title company will have to send a settlement agent who will represent them. It is this agent who will bring all vital documents, talk and discuss everything with the involved parties, collect the costs associated with closing, and distribute the funds.

In addition, the title company also plays an important role in ensuring that every new deed, title, and other essential document gets filed in a timely manner with the correct entities. A title company will also do the following for anyone who paid for their services:

- **Research about the chain of title** – This refers to the complete history of the ownership of the property/home. One search by your chosen company is enough to find out if there is a second owner, making it possible to stop the transaction before the actual closing.
  You can also expect these professionals to be of help in searching for existing liens, thereby preventing the risk of finding out only later that the contractor did not get any payment for any completed work they did for the home in the past. This means you can prevent anyone from asking for payment from you when you have just acquired ownership of the home.
- **Research the title and conduct a survey regarding the property** – The property survey is a necessity when it comes to closing a home in the majority of states. The survey can help ensure that the property occupies only the amount of space that the title indicated. It also benefits you as this will give you an idea about inclusions in the purchase – ex., if whether the fence of your neighbor is included on the property you bought.

Upon completing the research, expect the title company to give out a report known as the "title abstract". You, together with the lender, will receive a copy of this report, so you can review it before closing the home. Take note that the abstract we are talking about here does not refer to title insurance, which is actually another document that you should get from a real estate agent.

- **Determines who should hold the title** – Ensure that you are getting help from an expert title company that can make sure that every wording in the title provides an accurate description of who exactly possesses the right to transfer. This is important as how the title is phrased can have an impact when it comes to paying property fees and taxes just in case you intend to sell the property in the future.

Those who are single or not yet married will find this whole scenario easy considering the fact that the only name in the title would be you. This means that you have sole ownership of the title.
However, things may get complicated if you are already married or live in a state with community properties. It is in this regard that you will need the help of a title company who can assist and guide you in comprehending what is good for you as well as what to incorporate into the title.

A title company will indeed be a good help for property buyers who intend to close a sale without hassle. Hiring the services of experts who are behind title companies can provide you with favorable benefits but it would also be a great idea to operate your own. This means it would be a great idea to build and launch your own title company. What will you need if that is the case? The next part of this chapter will tell you.

Essential Requirements for Starting a Title Company

So are you interested in starting a title company now that you have heard of its importance in the real estate industry? A title company is definitely one of the most lucrative business ideas right now considering the huge number of people who may require related services.

Note, though, that you can't start it without completing and fulfilling the necessary requirements. Also, keep in mind that such requirements will vary based on the state you are in. In other words, you should keep yourself informed first about licensing the title company in the specific state you are in. You can also get started by reviewing the official website of the Department of Insurance.

It is crucial to understand the laws about starting a title company in your state as you will be in need of a license that the insurance division or department in your state will issue. Most states only award the license to a candidate who was able to pass the licensure exam.

Before doing that, though, it would be advisable to determine how eligible you are to start and operate this type of business in your state. In this case, you have to meet the eligibility criteria, which may change a bit depending on the state. However, most of the criteria also stay the same – the most common ones include:

- 18 years and above
- Ability to write and speak in English
- Legal residency in your own state
- Notary bond
- Passing rate on the licensure exam
- Course completion
- Should not have any criminal record in the past

Note that there are states that are very specific in terms of the mentioned points. For instance, in Florida, applicants for title companies have to meet the requirement of being non-residents in other states. This means that the applicant should only be a Florida resident.

Also, take note that while getting the license makes it possible for you to open up your own title company, some states deem that particular requirement incomplete. For instance, certain states, such as New Jersey, New York, and Florida may require you to hire a lawyer and have him sign the documents for closing. If you live in any of those three states, it is advisable to have a lawyer on your team prior to applying for the license.

To further help you have a clear idea of what you should prepare for when starting a title company, here are the key requirements you should meet and complete.

Pass the Licensure Exam

After reviewing the guidelines and requirements in your state, you have to take a course related to starting this type of business. Find out what course you should take that will help you run your title company effectively. Visit the Department of Insurance page of your state, so you can receive a list of educational organizations that are already approved.

Your chosen coursework should be that which will help you in preparing for the exam. Take a course that will provide students with a full overview of the inclusions in the actual exam. The class should also provide quizzes designed to help you in preparation for the exam.

One thing to take note of is that if you already work as a lawyer or have your own title company that is in another state, the coursework may be waived.

Once you have completed your class or course, it is time to take the licensure exam. Sign up for the testing organizations in your state so you can take the exam. The licensure exam will test your knowledge of the principles of title insurance, as well as general insurance concepts, real estate transactions, title exceptions, and title-clearing procedures.

Generally, you should get a score of at least 70 percent, which is the passing rate. However, make sure to check the requirements in your state regarding that, so you will know if it is indeed the minimum score you have to aim for.

To help you with the exam, you can also take several of the courses online that will boost your knowledge in this industry. The good news is that most of these online courses are accessible at reasonable prices.

As for the exam, expect it to be held in certain locations. For instance, in Florida, the exam will most likely be held on a military base. If you are in New Jersey, then there is a high chance that the examination centers will be in office spaces. One more thing to take note of is that there are also specific states that do not need any licensure or qualifying exam.

If that is the case, you will have to complete a training volume. Once completed, you can take a hold of your license, which may happen in just a couple of weeks. It also helps to evaluate your experience in the industry first. Note that it would be easier for you to start your own title company in case you already earned a law degree. The same is true if you already have a few experiences in the real estate industry.

However, for newbies in the industry, it would be much better to start by working for a reliable title company for several years before forming and operating your own. You will also receive proper guidance in case you work for a business related to the industry, like a lender or escrow company.

Select a Legal Structure

This refers to the specific legal structure you will be using for your title company. Register the name of your company along with your chosen legal structure with the State Secretary in the particular state where you intend to run your business. The most common options you have as far as legal structure is concerned include the following:

- **Sole Proprietorship** – As the name suggests, this business entity is solely owned by you. If you opt for a sole proprietorship, then every debt and obligation incurred by your business will be your sole responsibility. It does not also require any formalities for its establishment. You can set up the business and operate it anytime you are ready. It is beneficial because the setup is simple plus it is not that expensive to establish.
- **Partnership** – This legal structure is famous among those who are planning to operate start-ups or small businesses. This is good for you if you are willing to sign up with an agreement with your partners. It requires at least two people to establish your title company. Since you are partners, you will be sharing all the profits and losses that the business has acquired and incurred.

- **Limited Liability Company** – An LLC can be described as a business entity, which offers owners limited liability. In other words, owners of this type of business do not have personal responsibility for the financial liabilities and debts it incurred. Many opt for this type of legal structure when establishing a title company because it promotes flexibility in terms of management, limited personal liability, and pass-through taxation. However, it also has some drawbacks, among which would be the fact that it is not available in some states and the taxes required for self-employment.
- **C Corporation** – You can also opt for a C corporation, which refers to a business entity, which is independent or separate from the owners. In other words, your title company under this legal structure provides limited liability to all owners. Any liability and debt will not be the personal or sole responsibility of the owners. One downside of forming a C corporation, though, is that it will most likely be subjected to double taxation. Both the corporation and the shareholders, therefore, will dedicate a chunk of their profits and dividends to taxes.

- **S Corporation** – This form of corporation gives owners limited liability protection while letting them pass through any income they generated from their business to personal ITR (income tax returns). This is a good thing as it helps prevent double taxation. Note, though, that an S corporation has a few limitations – one of which is in terms of how many shareholders will be appropriate for this particular structure.

You need to pick a legal structure for your title company so you can register it. After registering, expect to receive the official Articles of Incorporation from your state or any other document based on your chosen legal structure. This is important, along with other documentation, once you also start to establish your banking account.

As much as possible, consult a lawyer when trying to determine the best legal structure or business entity that is suitable for the company you have in mind. You need a lawyer to help you in drafting the articles of incorporation or articles of organization. In addition, your lawyer will be of help in navigating the laws in your state, especially when it comes to naming your title company and registering it.

Keep in mind that naming laws vary from one state to another, so having a lawyer around is definitely beneficial for you. For example, there are states that require the name of the company to have "title company". Meanwhile, others do not allow the use of "company" in the name.

Find a Location/Space

You have to look for a space where you can operate your title company first before applying for a business license. This is important as you need to present a verifiable business address. Make sure that you choose a professional-looking space. Look for one close to other offices you intend to work with, like real estate offices, mortgage companies, and banks. This means it should be visible and accessible to your prospective clients.

Also, your chosen location should be large or big enough that it can accommodate not only your entire team but also your office equipment and supplies. One way to search for the best location for the company you are planning to establish is to browse the internet for office spaces that are available for rent. You can now find a lot of websites offering this type of service, giving you a wide range of options. Compare the prices of the different office rentals and read reviews before you make your final choice.

Secure Funding

Upon deciding to establish a title company, you may have realized right away that you need to raise and secure funding for its launching. The funding has to be secured, so you can keep your title company afloat, especially if you are just starting out. The primary sources of funds for your company would be personal savings, bank loans, credit card financing, and crowdfunding.

You may also secure your start-up funds with the aid of your trusted family and friends. In addition, there are angel investors that refer to those who are willing to invest in a start-up title company, especially if they feel and believe that its potential for attaining success and growth is high.

Register with IRS

The next thing you have to do would be to visit the IRS (Internal Revenue Service) for the actual registration of your business. Once you have registered, the IRS will issue the EIN (Employer Identification Number). This EIN is necessary as it is a requirement in several banks once you open up a business account with them.

The EIN is also a requirement in hiring employees. The IRS will use it in tracking tax payments from your payroll. Note, though, that if you decided to go for the sole proprietorship structure without hiring employees, an EIN will not be necessary. What you will be using, instead, is your social security number. This will serve as your TIN (tax identification number).

Business Bank Account and Credit Card

Another key requirement in starting a title company is a bank account for your business. It should be under the name of your title company. The good news is that once you have registered your business, you can easily open up a bank account. Just get in touch with your chosen bank and submit the documents they ask for, including the articles of incorporation, proof of address, and passport or driver's license.

Fill out the application form and ensure that every piece of relevant information they ask for is provided. Once you have completed the form and submitted all the requirements, you can talk to a banker about the needs of your business. Set a goal of building a good relationship with your banker. This will prevent you from having problems with your bank account, which is a truly vital element for your success.

Aside from the bank account, it is also crucial to have a business credit card. That way, you will find it easier to keep business and personal expenses separate. Apply for one via your chosen bank or an actual credit card company. Once you apply for the credit card, do not hesitate to provide all relevant information about your business, including your business name, address, and the type you are running.

It is also advisable to offer useful personal information, like your name, birthday, and social security number. Once approved, you can start using your business credit card in making purchases. It is also possible to use it in establishing your credit history, a vital factor if you plan to secure loans or get credit lines soon.

Required Permits and Licenses

The next thing you should do is to get licensed, meaning you should get all the needed licenses and permits, so you can legally operate your business. Your title company needs to be licensed by the state where you intend to operate it. It may also be necessary to have a fictitious business name or a trade name registration.

Several states also require some forms of security and surety bonds before granting a license. Aside from the state license, you may also need to make your title insurance company become a member of ALTA (American Land Title Association) or any other related state land title associations.

Some states also require title companies to get a hold of a sales tax or utilize a tax permit. Meanwhile, other states have their own licensing requirements specifically designed for corporations. You have to find out what business permits and licenses you have to get to operate your business depending on the state you are in. Get all of them, so you will never experience any legal problems as you operate your business.

Get Insured and Bonded

It is also crucial for you to get all the necessary types of insurance and bonds depending on the kind of business you decide to run and operate. Among the types of insurance and bonds that are perfect for title companies are the following:

- **General liability insurance** – If your business has this type of insurance, you will get coverage for any injuries and accidents that happen to your property. You can also expect this insurance to cover damage that your products or employees caused.

- **Professional liability insurance** – This is actually a requirement in most states. Also called errors and omissions insurance, professional liability insurance will offer protection in case you encounter a negligence claim. This type of insurance is so useful that you should get it even if you are operating your business in a state that does not require it. The reason is that it will protect you from possible beginner mistakes that you may potentially commit during your initial years of operations.
- **Auto insurance** – Get auto insurance if you are using a vehicle for business purposes. With this insurance around, you will feel at peace knowing that you have coverage for stolen or damaged cars or vehicles.
- **Workers' compensation insurance** – You need this type of insurance in case you decide to hire employees to help you in your business operations. It is useful in combination with general liability insurance as both can offer protection against accidents and injuries in the workplace. This policy also covers lost wages and medical expenses.
- **Business interruption insurance** – You will also find business interruption insurance useful as it provides coverage for lost expenses and income in case of the forceful closure of your business. The closure should have occurred because of an event covered in the policy.

- **Commercial property insurance** – Expect this to provide coverage for property damages and losses triggered by theft, vandalism, and fire.
- **Fidelity bond** – You need a fidelity bond as it offers protection from possible losses caused by misconduct or misbehavior from any employee. For instance, if someone from your company is involved in embezzlement or fraud, the fidelity bond will offer protection from the losses that result from it. This makes it necessary to keep in touch with the bond center in your state and request to have this type of bond.
- **Surety bond** – With the help of this bond, you will have a hundred percent assurance that your title company will continue fulfilling its responsibilities and obligations to clients. Your clients are also allowed to get their money back in case something happens to your company. If you decide to get a surety bond, take note that the cost is often around 10% to 25% of the net worth of your company.

Visit a surety company, which specialization is specifically on new companies of the same size as yours. You can also deal with a surety broker. In terms of insurance, you can always look for highly reliable and trustworthy insurance agents. Inform them about the kind of business you are operating as well as its specific needs and requirements. You can then expect them to recommend insurance policies capable of fulfilling such needs.

Marketing Materials

Once you have acquired and performed all the essentials and the steps needed to start your title company, you can open and launch your business. Make sure that you also have the right marketing materials, so you can start attracting customers and work on retaining them. Among the most useful marketing materials that a title company needs are the following:

- **Attractive logo** – Take your time designing your logo to ensure that it is truly appropriate for your company. Also, take note that the logo is the one that is going to be printed on a wide range of marketing materials, including business cards. You have to design it in a way that can attract your potential clients. It should also be made in a way that increases brand awareness and the trust of clients.

- **Social media accounts** – You also need to create your business' social media accounts. It should have the name of your company. You need these social networks, like Twitter, Facebook, Instagram, and LinkedIn to reach out to your target audience.
- **Website** – It is also advisable to have your own business website. This should provide your target clients with all the information they need regarding your services. You can also use it to gain their trust by providing legitimate details about your company, like your contact information and company history. Be very careful when it comes to designing your site as it also has an impact on how your target clients will perceive your company.

In addition to the marketing materials, it also helps to invest in software that you can use in running and operating your title company efficiently. Look for a kind of software that is effective in managing the operations of your title company. You can even go for those that can help manage important aspects of your business, like title searches and overall finances.

Once all of these are set up and acquired, you can finally open your business. By following all the steps and requirements in this first chapter, you can improve your position and the ability of your business to succeed.

Continue reading the next chapters of this book, so you can further arm yourself with everything you need to know to start and launch your title company.

Chapter Summary:
This chapter tackled the basics of starting and launching a company. It talked about the following:

- Title company and what it does
- Common requirements for starting a title company
- Overview of title insurance
- Licensing
- Marketing materials you need

Chapter 2 – Types of Claims That can Pop Up

One thing that you should know about running a title company is that there are various claims, liabilities, and risks that may pop up unexpectedly. No matter how much you take your time to establish this type of business, you still can't prevent some issues from occurring.

There will be a point throughout the process of starting and growing your company when you will be facing claims since you will be involved in a lot of important tasks. This is especially true when it comes to closing services for property owners and homebuyers.

As someone who is running a title company, you and your team will be responsible for issuing title insurance and collecting and holding money designated for escrow accounts. You will have a lot of tasks on your plate and you can't expect to fulfill all of them without any challenges.

For you to become a well-prepared owner of a title company, this chapter will give you information about the different liabilities, risks, and claims that may come up during the course of your business operations. It is important to be aware of these possible challenges as early as possible, so you will know what to expect before you ever launch your business.

Claims and Challenges to Prepare For

Keep in mind that during the entire process of buying a property, some things may go wrong, so arm yourself with information about these potential issues to keep yourself protected. Once a client asks for your services, here are the usual things that may go wrong and the problems that you may have to deal with:

Forgery, Fraud, or Illegal Deeds

Among the cases that fall under fraud or forgery are forged signatures of past owners on the deed as well as false impersonation. This can cause a problem as it may result in the ownership being contested. The problem is that we are living in a world, which is not completely honest. This means that you will always encounter some fabricated and forged documents.

There may also be illegal deeds that occurred in the prior deed. Even if the property's chain of title looks perfectly good and sound, there is still a possibility that the past deed was taken illegally. For instance, it could be a contract entered into with a minor, an undocumented immigrant, or someone who is incapacitated. If the one who signed on their behalf does not actually have authority, this may lead to a defective title.

Such issues may cause a problem for your company and your clients, especially potential homeowners. The reason is that they may negatively affect how enforceable the past deeds are. These issues may also affect both prior and present ownership.

Wire Fraud

In relation to the previous topic, there is also what we call wire fraud, which is now a widespread issue not only among title companies but also in the entire real estate industry. The reason is that real estate transactions involve the transfer of huge amounts of money from one party to another, which is why wire fraud is so rampant here. All parties involved in such transactions become one of the primary targets of criminals.

The problem is that a lot of home buyers and financial institutions continue to fall victim to wire scams, especially those related to the closing of real estate. One reason why criminals prefer to execute this kind of scam is that they can easily pull it off, especially if you consider how naturally hurried or often rushed the process of closing real estate properties is.

Many scammers also seem to have an easier time pulling off wire scams because it makes use of email, which is a common means of offering legitimate and reliable instructions in terms of transmitting funds during closing. You have to familiarize yourself with how this type of fraud works so you can at least set a few measures that will help protect your title company from it.

Basically, it works with the fraudster hacking into the PC system or email server of the lender or title company. The goal of the fraudster is to find out whether there is a real estate closing coming up. After that, they will email the financial institution or the buyer of the property with false instructions related to wire transfers.

If the financial institution or buyer follows the provided instructions, it will initiate the wire transfer, allowing scammers and criminals to move upon sending the funds or money. However, you should take note that in most cases, it is only possible to discover this type of fraud once the closing agent or title company informs the financial institution or property buyer about their non-receipt of the funds they expected.

Take note, though, that there are several ways to prevent wire fraud. One thing to do is to inform all the parties involved in a particular transaction how important it is to call back the title company first using a confirmed number, so the legitimacy of the received instructions about wire transfer in fax or email will be verified.

It also helps to do the following:

- Set a passcode together with the closing agent or the buyer of the property in advance – Use this along with the verification process and call back.
- Use encrypted emails – The encrypted emails should be used whenever the instructions for wire transfer will be sent.
- Ask the property buyer to verify the legitimacy of every instruction for wire transfer that they received. If they received it through email, require them to inform you first for verification purposes.
- Find the usual red flags linked to compromised emails – Some red flags to watch out for are poor grammar and emails sent beyond the usual business hours.

Aside from the mentioned short and simple tips, it is also advisable to educate the people who help you operate your company as well as your clients about wire fraud and how rampant it is in the industry.

That way, every party and your entire company will be able to protect themselves from such fraud. Keep in mind that your clients may be held liable in case there is a loss of funds. With that being said, it is crucial for you to be aware of these warning signs of fraud.

Undiscovered Liens

If you are still unfamiliar with undiscovered liens, then note that it refers to a legal claim, which can be attached to a real estate property, like a home. It can provide a creditor with an interest. There is a high possibility for it to get levied for certain things, such as credit card bills, spousal or child support, unpaid contractors, mortgages, credit card bills, and outstanding real estate assessments or taxes.

One problem with this is that any pre-existing judgment lien, which was identified after selling the home, continues to become a lien on the real estate property. This can cause further problems for the owner of the property.

Incorrect Execution

This problem, which occurs because of inappropriate or incorrect execution of the process, is a common claim due to several reasons. For instance, the issues could be an incorrect name, improper notarization and witnessing, and wrong description of the property.

You can also expect to encounter this claim if there are errors associated with processing documents. With that said, you have to train yourself and the entire team to process documents without causing any errors or problems with them.

Missing/Undisclosed Heirs

Note that whenever someone passes away, there is a high chance for the ownership of their properties to get transferred to heirs. However, there are instances when heirs are missing during the time of death. The problem becomes even bigger when they turn up after a while to file claims on the properties that they think are theirs but now, are already sold.

There are also instances when relatives and family members end up contesting the will for property rights. The problem with this is that such scenarios may occur after buying the property, which is why it may affect the rights of the buyer. This is something that you have to prepare for to protect your company and the rights of your clients. In most cases, you can get the protection you need from the mentioned situations if you have good title insurance.

Lending Problems

There may also be issues that may come out during the underwriting process. The problem with such issues is that they may also cause escrows to fail when it comes to closing. In case the potential buyer made a huge purchase on their credit card prior to closing, found out about additional debt, or faced difficulties when it comes to providing the necessary documents because of self-employment, there is a high possibility that the deal will not push through.

You have to build a good reputation when it comes to handling these unanticipated lending issues as such is the key to winning the trust of your prospective clients. With the help of equally trusted and reliable lending professionals and escrow officers, you can earn the trust of the buyer, which is good if you want them to listen to you. They do not end up making major purchases or financial changes during escrow.

Open Equity Lines

There is also what we call an open equity line that tends to become more widespread because of the boom of refinancing during the past few years. Open equity lines can be described as a claim that often originates from borrowers who decided to put their property on a first mortgage and decided to take an equity credit line afterward secured with the aid of a second mortgage.

After a while, the borrowers further go through refinancing while aiming to settle both the first and second mortgages from the proceeds. The problem is that in several cases, the open equity line ends up not being properly closed while the mortgage linked to it goes unreleased.

Closing Issues

Title companies are also prone to dealing with closing issues, the ones that arise when the borrower or buyer ends up suing all the parties that are part of the transaction. This particular claim significantly increases the number of claims in titles.

What Your Title Company Can Do

There are indeed numerous issues and claims that may arise as you are going through the process of running your title company. In this case, the ultimate thing you can do is to check the title to a property presented to you closely. You have to scrutinize it well and ensure that it is clear and indeed available for selling. You and your team should be trained in examining property titles and detecting warning signs that may only cause delays in the sale.

For instance, if you discover debts, such as outstanding liens or unpaid property taxes, then be careful as those issues can cloud the property title. It is possible to resolve such items by finding out if it is just a clerical error that can be corrected. Your company may also help in following up on the outstanding lien, so you can verify if the debts are settled.

The problem is when you are dealing with legal judgments and unsatisfied bankruptcy claims. The reason is that those issues are not that easy to fix. As someone who operates a title company, here are the things you can do to clear up the property title:

Perform a title search

Keep in mind that it would be impossible to continue the process of selling a home in case the seller has no full rights to selling a property. This makes it necessary to conduct a thorough title search. Train everyone in the company to conduct thorough research on public records as a means of assessing if there are legal claims on real estate properties.

Among the records that you should scrutinize closely are mortgage documents, deeds, marriage and tax records, and probate records. Such information will be of help in figuring out whether there are issues in ownership.

Take advantage of title insurance

Note that regardless of how much effort you exert to conduct an extensive search with the goal of detecting ownership issues, it is still possible that you may have missed a trivial detail that has a significant effect on the title. In this case, you have to make it a point to invest in an insurance policy for it. The title insurance will serve as protection from unknown defects in the title, specifically those that may only come out in the future even after you have diligently done your research.

You can invest in either of the two forms of title insurance – the owner's and the lender's, which is also called a loan policy. You can expect the owner's policy to provide coverage for the entire amount that the buyer paid for the property. This coverage will continue to have an effect even after refinancing and switching lenders. Meanwhile, the lender's insurance provides protection only on the financial interests of the lender to the home or property. The coverage is usually the entire loan amount.

Be in close supervision of the escrow and closing process

If you are operating a title company in the US, your title company will be responsible for handling real estate closings, including the execution of closing procedures and providing paperwork.

It is also part of your responsibility to manage the home sale's escrow account, the one holding the funds specifically designed for earnest money deposits, closing costs, down payment, and the amount needed for the actual home purchase.

Make sure that your title company has a solution that can make the entire closing process and the escrow account secure. Supervise the whole process closely. It would help a lot if you have a system for scheduling closing appointments based on your terms. You should also be able to use this system in signing and viewing documents before the last meeting. This is a great way to assess how clean the title is and if there is indeed no issue with all of the documents.

Be willing to settle claims

What will you do if you encounter some claims? Learn how to settle with the help of your insurance policy. For instance, if your team suddenly faces the issue of an undisclosed heir, use your title insurance. Also, take note that your title company is responsible for providing legal representation, which aims to investigate and validate unexpected claims. You may also have to work on settling the issue.

There are even cases when your company will have to pay as a means of removing defects in the title, such as a lien. Other things that you have to do may include handling legal issues, such as easements and providing compensation for loss in value caused by title issues associated with the real estate property involved. Make sure that you and your entire team are proficient in handling all these tasks, so claims will be easier to handle and settle.

Chapter Summary:

This chapter talked about the different claims and challenges that your title company may face as it continues to be in operation. It also tackles a couple of solutions to such claims.

Chapter 3 – Underwriters, Title Examiners, and Notaries

Three of the most important roles that should be filled within your title company are underwriters, title examiners, and notaries. What are their duties and responsibilities and how can you find professionals who fit these roles the best? You will find out in this chapter.

Underwriters and the Roles they Play

An underwriter refers to a professional in authorizing agents to create and draft policies for title insurance. You have to work with one if you plan to start a title company as this is the professional who is responsible for insuring properties from insurable defects. You can also expect the underwriter to be of help in assuming financial risks.

In case of unexpected legal issues with insured real estate properties, the underwriter on your team will be the one to work on defending the title and protecting the owner of the property from legal and financial risks. You also need the underwriter's help to check and examine the property title and ensure rights and ownership to a piece of land or property. They will conduct extensive research regarding the chain of title to find out if there are potential challenges to the ownership or rights of property.

With the help of your underwriter, you will find it easier to spot problems and issues with titles, among which are problems with the legal description, judgments and liens linked to a real estate property, rights of minors, unreleased marital rights, omitted heirs, and defects in the past deeds associated with the property's ownership chain.

Note that as a title company, you have to assure your clients that the titles are clean and clear. With that said, expect your underwriter to be really thorough when it comes to scrutinizing public records, including wills, marriage certificates, deeds, and any other document that the title searcher discovered. The goal is to detect the presence of defects that may affect the property rights of owners and fix them as early as possible.

Another thing that the title underwriter can do is gather data from other sources that are essential in resolving and fixing the issues discovered when they did their search. In addition, they will review and list any possible exceptions to the insurance policy based on the ownership chain.

These are policy exclusions that will be received by the owner for the real estate property. A few examples of these exclusions that are vital in property transactions are encroachments, easements, and a few restrictions that can affect the property.

All these duties and responsibilities make an underwriter a really valuable addition to your title company.

How to Find a Good Underwriter?

Now that you know the importance of having an underwriter for your title company, it is time to begin your search for a really good and proficient one. In most cases, you can recruit the right one for your company with the help of the following strategies:

- **Internal hiring** – This means looking internally or within the company for present employees who qualify for the role of the underwriter. Hiring internally is a good move because you will be assigning the job to a present employee who already knows how your business works. In addition, hiring within your company is a good way to boost the satisfaction and morale of your employees.
- **Referrals** – You can also take advantage of the referral system. It is time to seek the help of your network and ask them if they can refer someone who fits the role of the underwriter.

- **Professional associations** – You can also check out various professional associations, specifically underwriting associations in your locality or state. Be a member of these associations, so you can access their list or directory of members. You may check these directories to find out whether there is a professional and expert underwriter who meets your criteria.
- **Online job posting** – Post your need for an underwriter online. There are several online job portals that you can now use in finding and attracting effective and proficient candidates for the underwriter position in your company.

Now, the question is, what should you look for once you already start the hiring process? In most cases, a proficient and great candidate for the underwriter position possesses the following qualities, skills, and professional experience:

- Impressive analytical skills
- Underwriter certification – Make sure it is current.
- Excellent attention to detail
- Experience in real estate and other related transactions
- Impressive organizational skills
- Proficient and knowledgeable in regulatory issues

Once you have reviewed the application and resumes of the top applicants, you can start scheduling interviews so you can get to know them better. Ask questions that will help you gauge their ability to assess the risk linked to properties and clients, research costs of projects, especially those related to renovations, and render application decisions after performing management consultation.

Find the best person for the job by assessing their knowledge about the industry and their level of confidence as they answer your questions.

What is a Title Examiner?

Another great role that should be filled in your title company is the title examiner. This refers to a legal support professional whose main role is to provide assistance to lawyers when it comes to reviewing titles as well as scrutinizing public records. The goal here is to find out the title's legal status.

The title examiner is also part of the insurance, legal, and real estate industries. These are the areas where they have to use their skills in researching a property's legal status to find out whether it is suitable for selling.

Among the records that they would have to scrutinize are past sales records, official maps, and property titles.

Also called title searchers, title examiners provide essential services to anyone who plans on buying or selling properties. This makes it necessary for them to have solid knowledge and a proper understanding of the state, local, and federal laws that can be used for properties.

The duties and responsibilities of the title examiner also include determining the presence of a formal disagreement or a foreclosure about the property border, so it can be fixed before the actual sale. It is also under the duties and responsibilities of the title examiner to keep a record of their findings and then report those.

What Should You Look for in a Title Examiner?

How can you find the best title examiner for your company? Note that in most cases, employers who need a title examiner only ask for a high school diploma since it is considered the minimum requirement as far as education is concerned. However, you may also choose to hire someone with a bachelor's degree and at least a year of experience in the industry.

Once you start accepting applicants, you should remember that the best person for the job is usually one that has excellent communication, computer, and analytical skills. These are among the key qualities that you have to look for during the hiring process. If possible, look for someone who also has any of the following:

- Experience with or knowledge of writing and computing protocols as well as statistics
- Good decision-making and leadership skills – The applicant should also demonstrate impressive time management skills and a positive attitude.
- Ability to gather and compile information
- Excellent problem-solving skills
- Attention to details

Also, take note that while a high school diploma is usually enough, it would be much better if you hire a title examiner who has a bachelor's degree in business, accounting, business administration, or IT (information technology). At least a year of experience in the mentioned fields is also a big plus.

Notary Signing Agent

There is a high chance for your title company to succeed if you make it a point to hire or work with the best notary signing agent. You need the help of a notary signing agent who plays a major role in real estate transactions, including facilitating the process of closing properties. Note, though, that the specific activities that your notary signing agent can do will be greatly based on particular laws governing the state where you can find the property in question.

Now, you may be wondering what are the usual duties of the notary signing agent. One key fact is that a notary is necessary for any title company that is currently operating as it is the one that confirms the identity of anyone who signs the document along with their witnesses. In this case, you need the help of a professional notary signing agent who plays the role of a notary public that received special training when it comes to closing real estate transactions, particularly those that involve a mortgage.

Generally, this professional works after receiving the closing documents often provided by the lender. A few examples of these closing documents are mortgage and deed, promissory note, and settlement check. Once the documents are received, expect the agent to contact the buyer and seller and arrange a meeting. This is necessary for collecting and notarizing every required signature.

With the help of the notary signing agent, you also have an assurance that the settlement check will be delivered to the right party. Once all of these steps are completed, the notarized documents will be returned to the lender.

One thing to note about these signing agents, though, is that their duties and responsibilities are also subject to some state restrictions. The reason is that every state is governed by its laws when it comes to how much the agent can take part in the closing of the real estate.

For instance, if it is in Texas, the closing process as well as the signing of documents should happen in the office of the lender if there is a line of credit for home equity involved. It could also be in a lawyer's office or in the specific title company used in recording the documents for the loan.

There are also states, like Maryland and Indiana, that require those who are closing transactions in the real estate industry to hold a license. Even with the mentioned restrictions when it comes to dealing with the closing of properties, a notary is still essential for any title company as they will need help in notarizing documents.

There will also be instances when you will have to offer notary services because of the huge number of closing and mortgage documents requiring the signature or seal of the notary.

As much as possible, hire a notary signing agent for your company, someone who has a lot of experience and underwent specialized training when it comes to signing mortgage and escrow documents.

By working with an expert and experienced agent, you will feel at ease and more confident since you know that you have a team who knows exactly how to handle transfers of ownership.

Chapter Summary:

Here, you have learned about three of the most important roles or jobs you have to fill in your title company – the underwriter, title examiner, and notary. This chapter also discussed the things that these professionals do, what makes them important, and how to hire the right people to fill these jobs.

Chapter 4 – Title Fees and Title Insurance Costs

Whether your title company offers services for the home buying or refinancing process, there will be costs and fees involved. You will have to charge your clients based on the costs involved in insuring, modifying, and reviewing the property title. These are what we call title fees since the title refers to a legal document, which serves as proof of ownership.

Different Inclusions in the Title Fee

A property title provides proof of legal ownership. In other words, having a property title means that you hold all the rights of ownership to the property in question. This means that you have the right to develop, sell, transfer, lease, or occupy such property to a different owner via a gift or will.

Those who intend to sell a home, though, must make sure that they can present a legal title. The real estate title, in this case, is often transferred through a deed, which refers to a document that you can find in the public records in the locality where the property is.

This will involve some fees. As the title company, you will have to charge title fees that refer to a set of fees associated with the closing process. You need to charge your clients the appropriate title fee, so you can start evaluating, adjusting, and insuring the title. You will be using this in performing research on the title with the goal of finding out whether there are issues, such as liens or encumbrances.

You can cover a lot of costs under title fees – among which are the following:

Title Search

Of course, this is the most basic inclusion in the overall title fee that you can charge your clients. Note that being the title company or agent means that your job is doing a title search, which aims to look into various public records to figure out whether there are documents pertaining not only to the property but also to its owners.

Your search will also uncover any defects linked to the title that may only limit the ability of the owner to enjoy ownership rights completely. You have to search a number of records, like those related to property assessments, court orders, wills, tax filings, and land surveys, among many others.

All of these activities involve some money plus require some effort on your part, so you need to set a cost for the entire service. This price actually differs depending on the kind of property you intend to research. For instance, if the property involved is only a standard home, housing just one family, you can charge around $100 to $250.

Note, though, that if the title search is for a larger home or building, you can charge higher. Also, take note that while a lot of title searches can already be accomplished within just a few hours, there are cases when it can take several weeks. Factor that in when trying to set a price for your title search services.

Title Exam and Report

The total fee also covers the title exam and report. This is the fee paid once your company's title experts begin reviewing the collected records during the search of a title and identifying if there are encumbrances associated with the supposedly clean title. A few examples of potential defects that may exist are outstanding liens from properties, land survey boundary discrepancies, granted easements, unknown heirs who have potential claims to the home or property in question, clerical errors detected in the documents recorded, and any other problem that may jeopardize or harm ownership.

Expect all crucial results of the search and investigation to be itemized in the initial title report. This particular area involves a lot of tasks, so it is no longer surprising to see the title exam and report forming part of the entire title search fee.

Attorney's Fee

There are also several instances when a title company has to include an attorney's fee in the total title fee. An example is when the property has an unclear or complicated history. If that is the case, your company may seek the help of a lawyer or attorney to check and review the title chain. If the case of your client requires the help of a lawyer when it comes to providing a title exam, you can incorporate attorney's fees into the total cost.

Closing Protection Letter

Also called LPL, the closing protection letter is an agreement that your title company has to write as a means of protecting the lender just in case there are losses resulting from misconduct of a closing agent. You can charge this fee for the effort of your title company to draft the file or document.

Title Settlement Fee

Also called the closing fee, the title settlement fee refers to the amount you can charge your client for the administrative closing costs. As the title company, you have the option to list this fee as an individual cost or not. In most cases, the title settlement fee covers escrow costs like those involved in handling and disbursing funds.

It also covers notary and survey fees, deed preparation fees, and any other fees and costs associated with the title search. There are also cases when the attorney's fees will already be included in the title settlement fee. Depending on what forms part of the title settlement fee, the cost you will have to pay for this area may vary.

Search Abstract Fee

You may also include a search abstract fee in how much you charge your clients overall if you need help from a third-party vendor who will disclose to you every historical detail regarding the specific property ownership. You can include it in the records as an individual item. You may also incorporate it into the settlement fee.

Survey Fee

You will have to pay this fee to a third-party vendor who will be surveying the property and confirming the boundaries if necessary. You can choose to include it in the settlement fee you charge your clients or make it look like a separate or individual item.

Deed Prep Fee

There is also what we call the deed prep fee, which can be applied when a title transfer is involved or when there is a need to modify an existing deed. For instance, upon the purchase of a home, it is important for the deed to be transferred to the buyer.

It is also a requirement when planning to refinance, especially if there is a change in marital status or there is a need to add or remove people from the title. If there is a need for all these details, you will have to include this type of fee in the total amount you charge your clients.

Notary Fee

This is another inclusion in the title fee that you may have to charge your client. This refers to the amount involved in getting the help of a notary as a means of pushing through the closing process. There is also a cost involved in meeting the notary at a certain location, so the closing can be accomplished. The help of the notary is also essential when it comes to transmitting scanned copies and mailing physical copies to title companies.

Title Insurance

There is also what we call title insurance. It could be a policy for the lender or the buyer.

The title insurance designed for lenders protects the financial interest of the policyholder for the property in question against possible claims in the future. These claims are from those events that occurred before the closing.

Note that even if your entire team did everything to conduct a thorough title search, there is still a possibility that you have missed something. The title insurance can cover such defects in the title that your company was not able to detect during the search.

Title insurance is also a necessity in case a mortgage is involved to finance the property. In this case, the policyholder should pay the premium in the form of a one-time fee and should form part of the total closing cost. You can also expect the policy to continue working for the entire time the loan still exists.

There is also the owner's title insurance, which is an optional policy but highly recommended. Similar to the title insurance of the lender, the one for the owner offers protection from future claims caused by undetected defects and issues to the property title. The policyholder will have to pay a one-time premium to avail from this insurance. It will continue to be in effect throughout the time that the owner will have a financial interest in the home or real estate property.

Home buyers also have the option to extend the coverage. For instance, they can get coverage for the property's future value, especially because the usual title insurance protects them from possible losses that go up to the actual property's value during the sale.

Pricing

As someone who intends to operate a title company, you need to learn about how you should price the total title fee as well as the insurance. That way, you can charge your clients appropriately and even offer deals that they will find irresistible. One thing to note, though, is that title fees tend to vary from one company to another and from one state or location to another. The inclusions will also have a say on the actual amount that you will be charging your clients.

Generally, though, the closing cost where a huge part of the title fee will be taken is usually around three to six percent of the property's actual purchase price. Now, another question you may be wondering is who is responsible for paying the title fees. The answer will be dependent on the location. Some states or parts of the country require sellers to pay the title insurance of the buyer while the latter has to pay the lender's title insurance for the owner.

It is also the property buyer who will be responsible for paying title search and recording fees. It is, therefore, safe to say that the bulk of the entire escrow, closing, and title fees usually falls under the shoulder of the buyer when performing a real estate transaction. Only a smaller part or percentage of the entire closing cost will be covered by the seller. Note, though, that it is not rare for both parties, the seller and the buyer, to negotiate as to who should pay what in the closing cost.

Despite that, you and your entire team should have a specific system that will help you determine how you should appropriately charge each client. How much your clients must pay should depend on factors like the location of the property, the actual sales price, and the mortgage company or financial institution involved in the purchase.

A lot of title companies follow a formula when it comes to computing escrow and title fees. They usually use a typical base rate, which serves as the initial cost, after which, they will have to add a certain percentage for every thousand dollars of the actual purchase price.

In terms of title insurance, there may be additional variables that can have an impact on the cost.

These include regulations in the state, negotiations made by the buyer and seller, negotiations made within the policy's full components, and bundle discounts that are currently available.

There are also states with certain regulations on title insurance, like Florida. You can work together with property buyers to decide on the title insurance parameters for a specific property. In most cases, a thousand dollars per policy is considered the standard average for home sales.

Chapter Summary:

This chapter focused on the different costs that you can charge your clients. It tackled title fees and title insurance – both of which are essential in making the job of your team easier. It also talked about proper pricing and who often pays the fee.

Chapter 5 – How to Strategically Market the Business to Gain New Clients?

Now that you are aware of most of the things that will help you jumpstart your title company, it is time to do the most important aspects for your success in this business – marketing and promotions. One important thing you should remember when trying to strategically market your title company and gain clients along the process is that real estate agents serve as the best sources of referrals.

The reason is that they are the first ones that prospective buyers of properties find and approach whenever they browse and search the web for available houses and properties for sale. With that said, they are also the ones you should consider building a strong connection with, so they will recommend your title company to their clients and buyers.

When it comes to marketing your title company, your focus should be to build a game plan that will help you become more attractive to these real estate agents. By doing that, there is a high chance for them to recommend your services, work with you along with their clients up until closing, and offer support to your title company in case of future settlements.

Fortunately, there are several ways for you to gain the interest of more real estate agents, brokers, and lenders – most of which involve making some improvements and adjustments to your digital marketing technique. Aside from online activities, there are also offline methods designed to market your title company to lenders and real estate agents.

When drafting your marketing technique, start by thinking of ways to make yourself and your company more available and accessible to real estate agents in the industry. You have to expose your company, so the people you intend to reach will know about the services you offer aside from the fact that you are available to help.

To start with your marketing campaign, here are some valuable tips that will surely help keep you going:

Use the internet

In other words, you have to build your presence online. Note that having a solid professional presence online is the key to attracting more real estate agents and encouraging them to market your company. In this case, you need to create a modern, attractive, and professional-looking website.

Since it serves as the main point of contact for almost all of those who are interested to work with you, you need to exert an effort to make your website as interesting and professional as possible. Your website also needs to be updated and should be optimized for Google search based on the industry you are in.

One of the best ways to do that is to post interesting and fresh content on your website regularly. Be clear and concise when writing and posting content but ensure that it also has value, so you can continue grabbing the attention of your target audience. You also need to be clear about your philosophy, mission, and value. By focusing on making your website look professional and adding relevant and useful content to it regularly, it will have a much better position on Google. This can contribute a lot to increasing the number of agents who can easily find you.

One more thing that you have to do as far as going online is concerned is to be active on social media. By increasing your social media activities, you can increase the number of real estate agents who follow you. Your title company will, therefore, be on the top of their minds when searching for the types of services you offer.

You can give your title company more exposure by setting a target of posting two to three times weekly on one to two social media platforms. Just make sure that your posts are fun and educational, instead of salesy.

Create a list of prospects

After building a solid and robust online presence, it is time for you to create a list of all the professionals in the industry you intend to attract or target. Your list should contain the most qualified prospects. Since you are running a title company, what you should gather would be the names of the best real estate agents in your locality. Make a list of them and focus on introducing yourself to them.

For you to begin creating the list, conduct research on brokerages in the place you are operating. You may also check out real estate association groups in your locality and participate in them. Another thing that you can do is pick up your phone. Call local agents directly, so you can begin introducing yourself and the title company you are running. Several of these agents may be pleased to hear what you are offering, especially because they will always need the help of title companies.

Use publications

Each piece of media in your locality features a section designed for real estate at one point or another. You can take advantage of this as it allows you to obtain free press from the press releases and guest columns you made. It also serves as an effective and reliable means of getting noticed.

What you should do to increase the possibility of getting noticed by real estate agents is to buy advertising space in sections where they are most likely to view it. This can contribute a lot to exposing your title company to them.

Also, take note that even if a lot of publications related to the industry now operate online, there are still professional organizations and associations that are capable of providing a lot of title companies a boost in their reputation. Getting involved with an entity in the industry can help establish a better customer relationship, the kind built on trust specifically.

Take advantage of email

Now is the best time for you to begin collecting the email addresses from your network and contacts.

The reason is that email is still a very effective way of reaching out to the demographics you intend to target in a timely manner. What you can do is generate a single email that you can use to reach all of your contacts.

You may also use emails with specific demographics that you are targeting. One more thing that you can do is to offer access to links in the industry that demonstrate the value your title is capable of providing to your audience.

You can also use your email when it comes to executing an effective lead-gathering and nurturing campaign. Keep in mind that your title company will have a better chance of succeeding if you are diligent in capturing and attracting new leads and asking for follow-ups or updates from your present leads.

In this case, you can use CRM (customer relationship management) programs to attract and nurture leads. This program allows your title company to keep the information and details of certain clients, lead-related conversations, and sales calls in just a single place.

By using a quality CRM that you can operate through the web, as well as a properly defined process in terms of nurturing leads, you will have an easier time completing the process of gathering leads. You can also combine this with effective digital marketing and a professional-looking and attractive website so you can continue capturing leads and launch your campaigns that will nurture them through email.

Focus on getting files closed

If you are aiming to market your title company to lenders and real estate agents, then one of the best things you can do is to improve your ability to close files and make sure that this ability is recognizable whenever you present your company to them. Of course, you can't find anyone who is part of a real estate transaction and intends to keep the sale hanging without any movement.

You have to show that you are truly reliable to lenders. They should be able to depend on your company when it comes to doing due diligence during the title search, addressing all conditions and requirements that have to be met to get a clear title, organizing documents properly for closing, ensuring that every relevant document has a proper signature and notary, and transmitting the last set of files and documents to recording on time.

The goal here is to demonstrate the ability of your team to streamline the closing process, which is a big help in attracting repeat business. If you have never worked with a particular lender yet but a borrower picks you to perform title work, you should work on delivering a really good performance so you can show the lender that your services are worth using repeatedly.

Build your network

The goal here is to make your network as extensive as possible. Expand your network by constantly exposing yourself and your business to the right people around you. For instance, if you wish to attract the attention of a lot of lenders and real estate professionals, you should make it a point to attend networking and industry events, such as seminars and conferences, where a lot of them will most likely flock in.

Attending such events is an effective way to introduce the name of your company to a lot of people in the industry. You can also use such events in collecting emails from various brokers and lenders. Make sure that you are also creative when it comes to introducing your company out there.

For instance, you should keep your logo as vibrant and unique as possible to catch the attention of other people. Show how much you are interested in building a connection and network with them by sending a personalized email as a follow-up to the meeting.

Post relevant videos

In this case, you can use platforms like YouTube, which is famous for being the second biggest search engine right now. Consider marketing your title company and the services you offer through videos as such types of content are more fun and easier to consume and absorb compared to text.

As a matter of fact, more than 78 percent of online users watch videos on the web once a week at the very least. You can also add videos to your site. This is a good way to increase your ranking in search engines. Your social media pages are also among the best places to post your videos.

Focus on creating video content that is really relevant to the industry and make sure it talks about topics, like closing disclosures. Your video content should also be made in such a way that it showcases the best things about your company.

Use directory sites

Make it a point to take advantage of third-party directory sites, too. Some examples of these sites are Zillow, Google Places, and Yelp – all of which do not just usually rank higher compared to your website but also drive their own traffic. These directory sites also have their own star ratings and mobile apps. This makes them really useful for your exposure.
Consider having a listing with reviews on the mentioned directory sites. By doing that, it will be easier for your target audience to find your brand, which is the key to acquiring more opportunities for doing business with such people.

Grab opportunities for sponsorships

An example would be to sponsor events that your local Land Title Association may hold. Depending on where you live, there is a likelihood of you being a member of the local chapter or the state chapter of ALTA (American Land Title Association). Several states have their own branch of these associations that hold learning events, trade shows, and conferences from time to time. These events are intended for escrow and settlement providers, as well as real estate agents and professionals.

You may want to sponsor any of these events, so you can introduce your company to the professionals who will be attending those. Get in touch with the membership office in your state so you can be a member. Inquire about opportunities for sponsorship that may come in the form of business promotions using co-branded giveaways or events.

By doing these sponsorships, there is a high chance that the participants will recognize your services and brand one day. This means they will start thinking of you whenever they are in need of the type of services offered by a title company.

You may also want to start sponsoring community events. Keep in mind that the local consumer serves as your end customer, so you have to ensure that the members of the community are fully aware of the existence of your company.

They should be able to recognize your brand and the services you offer. It is possible to gain brand recognition and awareness if you sponsor community events linked to the escrow and title company you are running.

For instance, you may provide your services for a nonprofit in your locality. You may also choose to host or teach in a seminar or course intended for first-time buyers of properties or homes. You also have the option to sponsor sports programs and teams for the youth in your locality. By doing all these sponsoring activities, your title company will have a better chance of gaining consumer recognition.

There is even a high chance for you to receive opportunities for advertising in place of the support you offer to the mentioned events and communities. This can contribute a lot to promoting and exposing your business to your target audience, especially real estate agents and lenders.

Chapter Summary:

In this chapter, you have learned about everything you need to know about marketing and exposing your business to real estate professionals. It tackles the different ways for you to market your brand, boost brand recognition and awareness, and ensure that real estate professionals and lenders remember you whenever they need your services.

Chapter 6 – How to Expand the Business When the Time is Right?

In the last chapter of this book, we will tackle one of the most important indications that your title company is already a success – expansion. Find out if it is already the right time to expand your business. By learning about the signs that indicate that your title company is ready for the next level through expansion, you can take this important step more confidently. In addition, you will get to know more about how you can expand your business and ensure that you are doing it at the right time.

Is It the Right Time for Expansion?

Planning for the expansion of your title company is one of the most exciting moments in your life as an entrepreneur. It may involve plenty of work but the prospective benefits should motivate you to explore available opportunities. The first thing you have to do is to determine if the timing is indeed right.

I'm sure that you have already known by now how important timing is in the field of business. This makes it necessary for you to look out for signs first if it is indeed the best time for you to do a title business expansion. Some signs that indicate that expansion is already viable for your business are the following:

- You notice that your title business is already booming but you lack the resources to capitalize on it completely, thus, the need for an expansion.
- Your clients are starting to look for more products and services from you.
- You notice that the extra capital in your reserves is continuously growing.
- You have already outgrown your present location.
- There is a high chance of attaining more profits and benefits from growing your title company.

Aside from checking out if you already experience the mentioned signs, it is also advisable to decide on the title company expansion by answering the following questions and considering these factors:

What are your expansion goals?

You may find the answer to this question self-explanatory but note that there are several instances when the decision to expand to a bigger and newer market covers various rationales, among which are reasons related to revenue, like when you intend to build an extra line of income or revenue for your company. It could also be due to competition, which means the intention to take up or acquire a bigger market share.

Find out the exact reasons for your desire to expand first. By identifying your objectives for expansion from the start, it would be easy to isolate where the business expansion will be taken.

For instance, if your goal is to acquire a title company that is already in operation but in another new market, then it is highly likely that the volume of the transaction will be derived from the current book of business of the acquired company. Also, by answering questions related to the goals of the expansion first, you can perform an internal check and determine if such a decision is in line with the broader growth strategy of your entire title company.

Are there resources available for your business expansion?

The resources we are talking about here come in various types, including people (manpower), technology, and financial resources. You have to remember that expanding your business requires plenty of time. Some may think that it is easy to expand escrow and title companies since they seem to pop up in new areas and markets overnight. However, it is time to debunk that myth and realize the fact that the time you need to build a new operation is definitely significant.

You need to work with a whole group of people who should have the commitment to oversee and execute every aspect associated with the expansion – starting from licensing to finding and building the physical location. The expansion team also has to gather custom practices and requirements for the new local market.

Aside from the people you need in launching a new and operational title company, you may also have to hire a significant number of human resource positions to ensure that your business operation continues to run. Note, though, that you will find it a challenge to find and retain talent.

If you plan to execute a business expansion strategy for your title company, you should consider first if it would be necessary to hire new people on your team or if your existing team will already be able to deal with the expected volume of work apart from their present workload.

Regardless of the case, it will be crucial for you to spend time training the people you assign to navigate the new market. You have to train them so they can handle everything related to managing transactions depending on the customs and regulations in the locality.

Another key factor related to a resource that you should consider is technology. Keep in mind that for you to expand the operations of your title company in a lot of markets, it is crucial to take into consideration how scalable your technology is. It is crucial for your technology or primary workflow software to help your title company retain consistent operations without minding the city or state you are in. In addition, it should be capable of adhering to the requirements of your locality.

For instance, if the expansion requires you to invest in scalable technology or software, which allows the customization of documents as a means of meeting local requirements. Choose software that will let you retain similar base elements of the process and layer custom local elements, like custom state action tasks in addition to the base process. By doing that, the existing team will be able to understand the processes quickly even if it is for a new market. With that, scaling your operations will be a lot easier.

Do you have the capacity to invest?

You also have to ask yourself whether you are indeed capable of investing before you ever go through the business expansion process. Keep in mind that you can't expect to be profitable when you expand your business to a new market right away.

With that said, it is vital to determine the exact amount you should invest in the new venture or operation before the company reaches profitability.

Find out first if you are capable of handling loss or weathering the storm in the new real estate market without putting your whole business in a nasty situation. In other words, if your cash flow is not that good, it may not be a good idea to expand just yet.

Also, note that your overhead costs will also increase since these expenses are necessary for running the operations, like the HR, staff, technology, operating and office expenses, and any other costs. You also have to factor in everything mentioned during the cost-benefit analysis. One more thing that you should consider would be the economic influences as well as strategic planning both for the short and long term. By considering all of these factors, you will know whether the time is indeed right for expansion.

How to Expand?

If, after considering all the factors mentioned and answering vital questions, you have realized that it is indeed a good idea to expand your title company, you should work on giving it a go.

How should you expand and make sure that you grow your business? Here are some great ideas:

Spend Time Looking at Your Past

This means analyzing the past or previous results of your title company and making a critical assessment of all your strengths and weaknesses. Make sure that you also gain a clear and complete understanding of the specific area where you intend to expand. In addition, you have to know how you can maintain an edge in terms of competition.

In that case, you should raise these questions and provide truthful answers:

- Did you learn some lessons over the previous quarters? What are those?
- How did your business or company change from one year to another?
- What were the specific areas where your business showed and sustained excellence?

Set goals

The next thing you should do is to set goals while seriously aiming to meet them. The goals you should set for the expansion of your business need to be not only clear but also forward-thinking.

Remember that for you to attain success, you have to find out what particular parts of your company you have to develop so you can attain your goals.

Also, keep in mind that your own business expansion may not be totally the same as that of the company of someone you know. One example is when you perform the expansion by improving the footprint of your brand.

Work on increasing brand recognition

Keep in mind that your title business and brand have to go together. Work on increasing the visibility of your brand not only to existing customers but also to the potential customers you are targeting. You can make that possible if you consider the specific forms of advertising that are highly effective in reaching your target audience.

One example is when you are thinking of posting videos that have tips for relevant content or starting a blog. Work on improving your home page – after which, you have to optimize the content in your website for search engines. In case you have no website yet, build one with the help of a user-friendly platform. You may also seek the help of a web developer.

You can also increase brand recognition if you encourage all of your followers to help in promoting your brand. Build awareness of the presence of your title company by enticing clients to provide user-generated content, such as posts, photos, and testimonials. You may also sponsor or take part in posts.

Increase your activities on social media

Social media wields the highest power among entrepreneurs right now, so you have to make sure that you increase your activities on social media. The good news is that there are plenty of social media channels right now that are ready for use. These include Facebook, YouTube, LinkedIn, and Instagram. Ensure that you also have access to industry-specific social channels.

Use such channels to your maximum advantage. You can do that if you start publishing high-quality posts that a lot of people will read and click on. You can also increase your activities by being more active on your channels. It is possible to do that by replying to comments regularly. You should also start sharing and liking the posts of others.

Do not stop promoting, too, whether it is online or offline. Note that even if you are already running a business, you still can't expect your work to be completely done. You have to continuously work on staying current in the minds of your audience.

You should, therefore, continue to advertise your company along with the services you offer.

Also, find several novel means of doing business promotions both online and within the community you are in. If you have special features, offers, and promotions, send them to your audience in a timely manner via email, social media channels, or on your official website.

Be willing to share everything you know about the industry

Note that an effective means of getting your brand name out there and expanding your title company is to provide advice to others. You have to share your experience and expertise in the subject with prospective and current customers. It also helps to become a volunteer member of a non-profit organization.

The goal here is to leverage social media, especially when sharing vital information about your business. Some of the most effective means of conveying and spreading what you know in the industry are the following:

- Making an FAQ (frequently asked questions) on your site
- Commenting on web forums
- Submitting how-to content or posts online
- Offering insights regarding the trends in the industry

Consider your finances

It also helps to take your time in analyzing finances. Note that you can only attain success and retain that through proper budgeting. This means that before expanding your title company, you have to make sure that you are fully aware of the financial status of your company, especially in terms of income and expenses.

Your budget also has to have some room for unpredicted and unforeseen expenses. As you expand, keep in mind that it would be more beneficial for you if you overestimate costs or expenses instead of underestimating them. You should also set the goal of ensuring that the entire expansion truly has a good financial sense, especially for you.

Communicate with your customers

Your business will most likely succeed if you keep on communicating with your consistent and loyal customers. This means that you can retain them. In addition, you also have to learn about the kind of growth potential you will receive upon expansion.

What you should do is tap into your present customer base to determine the services they wish you would add to your current list and how much they are willing to pay for those.
You should also use your present customers to learn if expansion is indeed good for your title company.

Conduct market research by letting them answer surveys from you. You may send the surveys through social media channels or email and ask your customers to spend even a little bit of their time answering the questions in the survey truthfully. Another way to do this is to make your employees survey clients whenever they talk on the phone.

Build strategic partnerships

If you wish to expand your business, then you should consider looking for a company that matches your title company and operates in line with your values and principles. You should try to create informal yet strategic partnerships with those companies that offer services to the same client base that you have.

The goal here is to send business to both parties. In other words, you can send business to them while expecting them to send business to you in return. Make it a point to grab the attention of your clients and boost your brand. You can do that if they offer promotions or discounts.
You should also consider expanding your reach by networking with not only potential clients but also other business professionals. You can make that possible if you keep on taking part in in-person networking events, make contacts during special occasions and gatherings, and keep in touch with your past colleagues with the goal of maintaining a solid relationship with them.

Aside from helping you expand your business, the process of networking is also a good way to gather useful insights straight from other experienced professionals. You will be guided, especially if the professionals are those who were successful in expanding their business.

Chapter Summary:

This chapter tackled the signs that indicate that it is indeed time for you to expand your business. It will let you know the proper timing for doing the title company expansion and how you can make that possible.

Conclusion

It is not that easy to start and launch a title company. You will have to dedicate a huge chunk of your time, money, and effort to this business venture. Despite that, it is not impossible to build your own title company and run it successfully.

Hopefully, this book serves as your partner as you try to achieve success and attain your dream of running your own title company. I hope the contents of this book further motivate you to build your title company and begin its operations soon.

Good luck!

Made in United States
Orlando, FL
14 November 2024